on my mind

a few thoughts from jude mcpherson

blacoetry press
versailles-frankfort-lexington

Published by blacoetry press
Lexington, KY
www.blacoetrypress.com

Text copyright © 2007 Jude C. McPherson

All rights reserved. No part of this publication may be produced, stored in a retrieval system, or transmitted, in any form or by any means, electronic, mechanical, photocopying, recording, or otherwise, without prior permission of the publisher.

Library of Congress
Cataloging in Publication Data
McPherson, Jude
on my mind
I. Title
ISBN Trade 978-0-6151-4286-9
Published June 2007
1st Printing

Photographs by Tracey Doyle

All praises to the McPherson and Franklin clans, the Doyle family.

Teri Hamilton, Shannon Ritchie, Teri Morford, Matt Merrill, Kyle Fanon, Deanna Dennis, The Affrilachian Poets

K. Nicole Wilson, Lerin Kol, Carrie Deaton.

And a special shout to my click. All of you have been there through the madness that is my life. Tracey Doyle, Bianca Spriggs, Ron McPherson, Eric Sutherland, Hillary Bobys.

This is yours as it is mine.

the poems.........

instruction 11

first 12

wax 13

a bookseller's manifesto 14

egoing becase i can 16

ever 18

fins 20

anniversary 21

exit/us (goddess dub) 22

hip hop is 25

immersion 30

air 35

rooftop 38

sunrise 39

meaning 40

a thought 42

a bluegrass interlude 43

break room meditation 44

a volt in the hand 45

loku # 1 46

loku # 2 47

writers block or hillbillies and b boys 48

8:13 am 50

affrilachian 51

6 lines 52

in transit 53

lunar 55

sweetwater women 56

comes and goes 57

red 58

oh, by the way 59

southern women 61

push the panic button 62

psalm one 67

psalm two 68

hair 69

waiting room meditation 71

on my mind pt. one 72

J 0 493 75

kentucky i'm doin fine
best kind of women and corn cob moonshine
not sayin y'all yankees aint got it good
wouldn't leave the bluegrass if i could
'cause i've got kentucky

-craig russell

instruction

start
everyday
with
a
hellabig
bowl
of
cubed
peas
and
a
glass
of
verbs

first

i am
you
the pause
taking the pulse
of infinity
between breaths

wax

(for Chris Buxton, the man who sold me
my first hip hop record)

so i used to raise up
on saturday mornings
shake the cobwebs from my head
and
make the pilgrimage
into a bears basement cave
where this beast of peace
would share his
profuse wisdom of sound
that would remove
the wax from my ears
so i could hear clearly again

a bookseller's manifesto

(meditation working at joseph-beth booksellers)

it's 2:00pm
it's saturday
two days from now
santa comes breaking and entering
into more first world homes than ever
tongue kissing wives
and we wonder why you can't say the word sex
without people in the social sciences section
lowering their heads like so
still believing that birth was somehow
¾ puritanical well wishing and ¼ stork

in droves they come
plastic razors in hand
slicing their veins at 18.7% six month introductory rates
meaning the whole concept of debt
has now replaced baseball
as the great amerikan pastime
that enters through a wall
mack truck ton of bricks like
the wind that swirls and cries and screams

like people at parties trying to ascend

vocals of natural selection above the biosphere
of techno suicide notes dipped in ecstasy
we hang name tags around our throats
so mr and mrs i-just-bought-a-mercedes
bow-to-me-and-cater-to-my-every-need
and-show-me-where-the-$35-hardcovers-that
i'll-never-read-are-located-you-indentured-servant
can know our names
and then it occurs
when poets tongues gallop through the countryside
proclaiming that the redcoats are coming to dinner!!!
to reclaim new england for old england
in the name of bloody cows jumping over the moon
beaming the light of knowledge as it has been known
to exist in some mythological in some realm
right next to arks of contemplation
holding commandments that remind me
that it's wrong to key someone's benz
in the parking because they cut you off
and took your space you savored for so long
now i wonder how long
until the announcement is made
and everyone's exits and brings me
just a taste of quiet
and something worth reading
tomorrow as i'm hitchhiking
searching for a ride to work

egoing because i can

i'm a pretty boy
though nothing about me
is textbook beauty filled

i'm pretty because my head is big
naah mean? phat as hell
my organic aesthetic
is 180 from pathetic
my big baby greens
absorb the jealousy
fingers pointing
at the vastness of my skull
and mighty brain matter
but that don't matter
they just mad my head
gets more attention than theirs

i don't acknowledge
cosmo created definitions
of what pretty is
for my definition is homegrown
watered by j-u-iced vocal throbbings
sprouting saplings so stank
loving them
is an admission of madness
i'm a pretty boy

though nothing about me is
textbook beauty filled

i am a pretty boy
with a serpent mound round belly
and a pair of vast soup coolers
that look to blow flows
into microphones with vocal tones
tall tales so ego tripping they dripping
from speakers to audience ears
that eventually comprehends the truth

i am a pretty boy

ever

(for wendy wells and herve' antoine)

on front porch swings
that creak with character
and the sounds of tall tales being told
quiet breezes have a way of stirring the soul
and this is what matters

Renewal

marriage isn't easy
being single wouldn't even be a consideration for most
if all it took was saying 'i do'
it's a painting forever in progress
crafted by two kindred beings
who trust enough to follow one another's brush strokes
carving into souls colors that sing in the key of eternity

you must be relentless in your love
wield embraces and kisses like pen to paper
and scribble in your hearts margins a manifesto of faith
in a language only you understand
that generations will celebrate after you have gone

you must be a farmer in your love
plant seeds of spiritual offering into this garden
turn the soil with daily conversation

water these plants with promises
sanctified with the blessing of sun and moon
then walk though hand in hand
watching your legacy grow

you must immerse yourself in your love
wear each other like suits of armor
and overwhelm all around you
with the endlessness of this day
for your 'i do' is proof
a continuing answer
a new chapter to read over and over
while sitting on porch swings
stirring the air around you
with the breath of two souls
renewed as one

love

fins

(a meditation at a jimmy buffett concert)

for amusement's sake
i decided to fine tune my baby greens
and set them on a pirates mission
to count the colored faces
among this sea of alcohol soaked
parrotheads that have descended upon riverbend

from cars full of characters
to truck beds filled with sand
to busloads of white folk
longing for a three hour escape
from the grind of everyday
they come downing margaritas
murdering beach anthems
decreeing the divine nature
of sponge cake
cheeseburgers
and rum
as i stand knee deep in swells
swirling with coconut bras and grass skirts
asking my cohorts on this mission
'does it count if they're on stage?'

anniversary

(for the affrilachian poets)

we are nothing more
than souls in transit
an amalgamation of spirits
sailing on seas of ideas
vocalizing endless beats of breath
with and without mics
amplifying every word
until it's heard
by everyone not listening
for we are one
poem
still being written

exit/us

(goddess dub)

for tracey-

i parted these waxed lips far enough
to struggle over broken & bruised syllables
piecing together a disjointed symphony
of an answer for your question

what are you thinking?

i'm thinking that the looking glass
now swallows the silver threaded confessions
that i want to reserve for your cochlea
of how i'm beyond discussions
of past present future
the only time is now
and now i cup soldier's hands over my ears
trying to stretch the resin
of homegrown Kentucky woman tongue
a rocks throw further
because walking this rock alone
has become walking this rock lonely
when you're not here to teach humility

i'm thinking that hearing you
while your face cradles my temple
is jah speaking full circle
deconstructing the disillusionment of pain
erecting in its place a voice
lifted from mama nature's southern favorites
that smells like Woodford county mornings
tastes like elation on the first saturday in may
and speaks truth like dem old' heads
rooted to front porch rocking chairs
that creak and crawl come summer time

i'm thinking of a shining star
how you delayed your departure from my nest
for seven hundred and twenty-two seconds
that we bent with poets tongue
wrapped the very essence of our meeting
while taking patient turns providing respiration
inhale 2...3...4
exhale 2...3...4

i'm thinking of august
and how the sun hangs on the wall
crossing/popping like b-girl stance
tagging face/cheek/tongue
with nappy headed naturalness
touching my green mirrors
i blinking remixes
her organic needles pausing their ascent

long enough for turntables to rub bellies
inhaling ra cooked kentucky earth
basted in a confederacy of
sweat
saliva
sex
symbiosis
conceiving a star crossed agrarian legend
of how dreads and bald heads
go together
like beans & cornbread

i'm thinking of osage orange trees
and rooftop beginnings over the elkhorn valley
and how in times of drought
i try to summon your resin back to my tongue
and irrigate my field of existence
with your country woman's grammar
drifting to never never lands in backyard hammocks
caring not who sees us fade away into each other
disappearing from this landscape one breakbeat at a time

i'm thinking of you

hip hop is. . .

hip hop is a spray can
cannon/balling and shot calling
from brick and mortar shanty towns
to sanitized suburbs
where kids a million shades
trade mix tapes all day
accepting new beats with head nods
giving one another pounds
uttering something like
'big ups'
or
'holla at your boy'
or
'word'

hip hop is the beat
bombing the inside of brain matter
with discussions of who's phatter
jigga or nas
the block is hot when five-oh pulls over
anyone with 808 in the trunk
countless rapes and robberies all around town
and you're giving me a ticket
just because i wanted to bump?

hip hop is a history lesson in progress
you can't claim true head status
unless you overstand
the future of hip hop culture
is in the past
commercialization of the art
and
racist interpretations of the future
are part of the assault on the word

hip hop is language
some
say it
sounds like
some
sophomoric
silliness
simpletons
speak
and that's
sad
it's a global vernacular
as spectacular as any verse
that spills from byron or billy shakes head
language is freedom
and hip is a spoken manifestation of this truth
or as calvin broadus would say
'for shizzle'

hip hop is dedication
i knew the words to the message
before i learned the pledge of allegiance

hip hop is death
part of a generation's hearts broke
when biggie and pac faded
they were never a threat
to become a synonym for perfect
but they were ours
and for hours i would kick back with phat sacks
packing blunts like samsonite suitcases
passing to whomever
was present and participating
and ready to head nod to breakbeats
from the streets of l.a. and n.y.
and i still sometimes want to cry
when taking communion
contemplating the brief union
of two black shining souljahs
taken away much too soon
now death looms when violence increases
itchy triggers from my peoples pieces
decreases the likelihood
that hip hop will survive long enough
to have a golden age
and the rage that boils within me
offends me because black on black crime
solves nothing that

couldn't be solved with a battle rhyme
but i guess it's not hard enough
if all you do is call your style tough
even fisticuffs would be
preferable to heaters clapping
so when i hear about so and so beefing
i don't even want to know what's happening
because i've seen where it's going
once all positive thought has evaporated
and hate keeps snowing

hip hop is representing where you from
i aint from brooklyn or queens
i aint from south central los angeles or oakland
i'm from woodford county/the 120/versailles, ky
holding it down like gravity/don't be mad at me
because i call home the dub c
i remember back in high school
banging beat after beat
on lunch room tables & walls
trying to sound taller
in hallways with ample freestyle skills
to kill any thought my belief is not real
feel me?

hip hop is life
spliced with living exhaling
breath into microphones
giving nouns, verbs & adjectives

homes in your eardrums
for the sum of all things i do
seasoned with hip hop
everything i know
everything i see
everything i flow
everything i believe is hip hop
don't believe me?
just look at the writing on the walls
and all the mics that i've ripped
just be careful of the
empty spray cans on the ground

you just might slip

immersion

i want to bathe in your words
every seismic syllable
that spills from your lips to your hips
can shower me
like a mississippi summer tempest
seeping through cracks and crevices
in the mornings allied armor

you can call me coltrane if you want to
because i play make believe
saxophone serenades to the night
hoping they find they way to your eardrums
and make you hum along
head nodding to the riffs i'm laying down
boooo deee doooooooo
booo doooo doooooo doooo weeeeeeee oooooohhhhhhh
boooo doooooo dooooooo weeeee oooohhhh

and every time i see you
i want to flee with the moment
because i feel high like the wind and i flow mine
i make yard sale wind chimes
keep the correct time
while they jingling and jangling
untangling a coronary conspiracy
are you hearing me?
it's older than day/seven days older than night

that came into being
when the cosmos said it was right
right enough to whisper
frank walker and kelly ellis verses into your ears
while we slow dance in a gravel parking lot
under shrouds of makers mark mosquitoes
and
half blown neon signs
advertising open mics
inviting me to represent right
right enough to have old players
sipping bourbon in the crowd
waving glasses in the air
inhaling vapors from kools and ports
that makes love to our costumes
while sisters tell them
to sit they drunk asses down
because a black angel
is looking for his wings
and that's what i sometimes aspire to be
a mahogany angel that lays on the page
mushroom clouded fantasies
of fucking your mind
with a billion unrehearsed verses
being voiced by my voice
that wants to tap you
like a sugar maple
and savior your flavor
that's somewhere between

candied yams and
the taste of sour mash on my tongue

and since i have your ear
i hope you don't mind me asking
do you feel it coming yet?
and if you do you can understand
this more than natural progression
form temptation to confession
and right now i'm confessing
i'm on bended knee
pleading my case to the goddess
for i have sinned and will sin again
if it means replaying
the contorted metamorphosis
of an earthbound consciousness
with the ascension of an angel
who
is
spinning
and
spiraling
somewhere
in
space
sucking
and
singing
leaving

sweat
laced
signatures
at
the
end
of
sensual
sonnets
sweet
like
honey
bees
seeking
sublime
simplicity
something
southern
and
countrified
like a woodford county tire swing
swinging a crickets leap
above nappy bladed grass
and every time i swing
this soup of southern love
pierces my soul with all the questions
i hoped would have answers
questions like

excuse me, but where's your man at?
does he know you're here?

air

no bird soars too high
if he soars with his own wings
-william blake

i have dreamt that i somehow was you
but even in that never never land
where physics becomes clay in the hands of children
you were you
and i was an awe struck seven year old
skipping my words broken record like
how did he do that?
how did he do that?
how did he do that?

your mere presence on this earth at this time
is proof that poetry is real
you
the synonym for swagger
you the living metaphor of love
you
the antonym of losing
you the reason a generation of little girls & boys
believe that humans can fly

time ceased to have any relative meaning
when from the wing you spread your wings
and ascended into a perception

of reality only you understood
suspended yourself until all others
succumbed to the biology
that they were a little more susceptible
to issac's notion of gravity
than you were

not even summer tarred hills could hold you captive
a carolina boys powder blue armor
gave way to the paradox of a bulls red
but that number twenty-three held strong
no man of steel
but a man of steel will
folks proclaimed a second coming when you ascended
'second coming of what?' i wondered
you filled a void the size of a tobacco road sunrise
no one knew was there

doctors with webbed hands no longer pack blowout combs
and leap house to house finger rolling prescriptions

indiana seeds come man don't rain shamrocks
on parquet gardens in the spring

spartan boys don't grow to be magicians no more
flashing smiles like a paparazzi
of purple & gold no look passes

you are simply you
whatever absurd height you raised the bar to
you cleared
legs spread
mahogany arms ascended into our souls rafters
a bull toying with matadors
your tongue taunting

like mike/if i could be like. . .

rooftop

i see
a red
steel
gliding
rocker
moonlit
exhalations
two peas
looking
to see
the stars
tonight

sunrise

. . . then slowly
like a pot of mustard greens simmering
the earth twists on its axis
and this once around midnight canopy
starts to give at its seams
as the first pink & purple fingers of jah's hands
reach from home
and delivers the proclamation
that there should be light
here

gulls of three beat wings
upon the suppleness
of mornings
adolescent
elastic
spine
singing a
symbiotic tune
while the noise of pickups
on the way to work
explodes in the background
always sounding off key
but still playing the same

meaning

i am thinking
that sometimes my words
are meaningless

can't seem to stretch
the syllables around me
to make the thought police
go back to where they come from

can't seem to find the words
that can stand on their own two
under the creamy blue sky
my eyes want to roll back
into my head and i ask 'why?'
why does the pungent smell of flesh rotting
crawl from the speakers
whenever the cable news net\work is on?
why is it when the world (be)trayed centers fell
my gut started to burn with the reality
that life for colored people
around the world just became harder

and please forgive me
for my meandering
through your thoughts

hoping that someone
has found a piece of meaning
but i always find that
no one has found meaning
until you understand
if you don't like what i say
fly away. . .fly away
but even when i fly away
i somehow become a p.o.w. of rhyme
but i have no time for this
the right side of my cerebellum starts to itch
and persist with the thought
that no original thought exists
but even those words
have lost their meaning
know what i mean?

a thought

...and
the universe said "no" just to spite me
to illuminate her point
she wielded fingertips like brushes
and painted the sky a million shades of gray
just because i asked
"will you make the sun shine today?"

a bluegrass interlude

i sit quietly

absorbing the sounds
of unseen birds
footsteps
and
the sway
and swagger
of
summertime

breezes this stretch of year
are fly paper sticky
baptizing skin
in sweat tinged proverbs
well into the night
before giving way
to the blessing of
cool morning canopies

i greet quietly

break room meditation

break room silence
is broken by
booted beat downs
being given to concrete
below our third floor perch
mercury in thermometers
are seeing red today
the threat of triple digits is real
as the sun leans against our skins
indiscriminately blistering and burning flesh
in the name of summer

a volt in the hand...

thermometer is whispering to me
says that it's going to be so hot today
that dogs will chase cats
and they will both be walking

this i accept as the gospel truth

from b-boy to bucket truck i descend
for eight hours i trade my credentials as m.c.
for the responsibility
of making sure
the lights will burn tonight

loku #1

    a

          dead

          wire

    could

        lead

                   to

      death

loku #2

voltage

                                      equals

respect

writers block *or* hillbillies and b boys
(for gurney norman)

my poets tongue
became tied some time back
for reasons i hope jah
will help me understand someday
no longer understood how other scribes
made the ink spill and ride across the page
in a cadence whose warrior spirit is so similar
to the sounds that hillbillies and b-boys make
when sharing the art
lost feeling for the craft of
penning
poetic
paragraphs
punctuated with five mics worth
of thoughts that have been tick tocking
inside my head since '75

sitting at the feet of old heads
is a privilege that comes with the responsibility
of opening one's soul to elder eyes
if you are not willing to
give what you've
got you
get nothing in return
so when it's my turn to share
i quickly look to toward the sky

pray
before unleashing a brief work of fiction
into the classroom air
each passage reviewed
through our conjoined exhalations
until the tale can stand tall on its own

you learned me
bite by bite
how to feed myself
from a thick soup of letters, words and breath
tended to by front porch magicians hands
that knows the cure for writers block

8:13 am

the sun is finishing its stretch
while the coolness of morning
   laps at the exposed skin
   not yet covered in sweat

soon its rays will slap like pimp
laying its claim as the end all
but it's still a couple of hours
until i begin to bob and weave

affrilachian

a
herd
of
buffalo
assume
human
form
to
share
the
word
the
heard
has
created

6 lines

i choose
what to write
on each lonely line

               you choose
               to listen to
               whatever you hear

in transit

the wheels on the bus
go round and round
pounding
pavement on goodyear tread
these land worms
crawl all over town
looking for those down to ride
with minimum deposit

sitting slouched in splitting seat
penning diatribes between potholes
making this land locked ship
rock forth and back
pen
jumping

                                                    all

over

                              page

but
thought
stays
the
same

everyone on this bus
has entertained get rich schemes
to stack bread to the ceiling
and ball uncontrollably

but the growls of combustion
reel us back into the reality
that the odds of being on this bus tomorrow
are more likely than matching
lotto numbers
come wednesday or saturday

lunar

how you do that momma moon?
stretch invisible legs like they organic skyscrapers
being circled by angels dipped in gold and honeysuckle
making offerings of wings stretching from our lips
milky vapors baptized in seas of tranquility
in the name of ma, pa, and the holy we

from the top floor we look
elevators of consciousness
bowing to the way you sway
us over still waters
resurrecting ebbs/flows
while lazuras dances slow waltzes
from treetop to treetop
bullfrogged bass lines
rattle lumps in our collective throat
we write quiet quatrains
that name you
as the greatest show in the universe
tonight

sweetwater women

when ma nature
held seeds in her hands
she said a prayer
into the ears of the universe
then placed you
one-by-one
into earth
that had been colored scarlet loam
from spilled blood
and
spent sweat of ancestors
long since physically departed
from this plane
she then cupped her hands
and scooped sweet water from the cosmos
and rained you into existence
to inhabit the universe
long before man/child was conceived

comes and goes
(for the gulf coast)

the sun ascended to heaven
and cried infinity
the moon fell to earth and shattered
those who were there to see it
still say a celestial kaddish when night comes
wailing and testifying
pouring out liquor on asphalt hills
spitting in the dirt sighing
growing old
remembering love

red

i
sometimes
blush
poems
when
i
walk
into
rooms
i
know
you've
been
in

oh, by the way. . .

i am saying goodbye
the only way i can

unrolling

every letter
of every syllable
of every word
of every sentence
of every stanza
of every poem
so all that will remain
is the line i began to carve
some time ago

this monolith
as it has become
has grown as a child
overcome with curiosity
sometimes pausing its pilgrimage
on the corner of euclid and limestone
turning itself around
squinting into high beams
hoping to catch a glimpse of it conception
at times it has felt as an orphan would
in and out of foster homes
earning the uncouth reputation of problem child

who would behave
with immaculate posture
all the while wearing a mask
that is a museum of pain
filled nursery rhymes

but what is left
when all that can be cried about
has been cried over?
what is left when adolescence
was watched from a nosebleed distance
surrounded
by a fistful of voyeurs?
the ash that dances
with embers above cataclysms
now howling mad like lunar children
they seek to strike out into the world
not with anger of what had been lost
but with a covenant of joy
over what has been found
while rolling letters
into syllables
into words
into sentences
into stanzas
into poems
i forgot to read to you
when you were here

southern women

i've sipped on your words
thirsty or not
from womb to now
bathing in the afterglow
of woman hands
country black
copper red
cloud ivory
lemon yellow
honey brown
woman hands
whittling this boy out of
southern trees
you helped to plant

push the panic button
(the impeach the president remix)

and they said that when planes fall from the sky
the end would soon come
and from rodeo drive slums
the natives run
with seven figure incomes
into the sun
generating and regenerating
the baby boomers hope
of the old way of life
delivered to your living room
free of charge with a
self addressed stamped envelope
more than ready to envelope
kodaked reprints of future events

the television documents
manufactured visions of human beings
falling
with nero screaming behind them
whipping a chariot pulled
by 40 mules with no acres to plow
as we sit in our homes
stroking remote controls
pushing buttons trying to tune
into channels
that thoughts should not reach

coming to the conclusion
that we can't comprehend
why they don't want us there

folks say it takes a village to raise a child
we make it a practice
to expose our seeds to hades and its minions
everyday in our classrooms
where instead of peace and coexistence
manifest destiny is the flavor of the day
but the truth i like to spoon feed
to the youngin's hard heads
is that pledging allegiance
has nothing to do with patriotism

right outside the front doors
hood heroes and po po banditos
try to hijack our futures
while i pen from a lextran
a manifesto i clutch in me fisto
like a pistol
holding it next to the ear lobes
of those who refuse to listen
whispering in my scribbles
'hands up.. we've come for what's ours'

and what's ours is what we don't
appreciate enough to ride and die for
images on the news bombarded my psyche

with views of non-white hued folks
choking from second-hand gun smoke
taking a toke of this reality
shows the fallacy of life in the bubble
we spend our days
belly aching about two dollars a gallon
they bellyache because of shrapnel and/or hunger
now i can't help but to wonder
when it will be our time
to look pestilence in the eyes and dance
because the universe
has made sure that death is certain
and that no empire lasts forever

i wait while pretending that some truth is left
saplings of hope reinventing themselves
searching for a ray of hope
in a world where psychosis
contributes to status
heads of state choose sides
like touch football games
while populations pray
that it doesn't come down
to a hail mary to decide salvation

morning comes on the backs of hawks
circling on the collective cerebral currents
still gestating in the womb of our souls caverns
that echoes the foundations of eternity

this is a new day in an old world
and we are forced into having conversations
that can only be justified
by a divine sense of humor
do we still stand steel willed
rooted like the live oaks
scraping grey/blue skies
or
give in dropping to our knees
throwing our arms zions way
screaming through apathy and silence
"why have you forsaken us?"
only to be answered by no one

now everyone is looking
for a button to push
because everyone is looking for an addiction
some affliction
that transcends earth's jurisdiction
glowing from all the friction
escaping the old world
with newly penned editions
documenting the inhumanity
of the human condition
while daughters and sons
husbands and wives
friends and lovers
are sent on missions
because a shrub is a coward

and will never listen
to the writing on the wall
watching planes fall
into world trade sinners
just in time to pacify our hunger
for it's our last supper
of life as we now know it
so kick back and enjoy the ride
because we all have dr. strangelove in our rearview
riding hell all the way to earth running from a sky

that has never fallen fast enough

psalm one

the
sound
of
the
beat
tapping
on
eardrums
that
can
now
see
what
it
is
that's
being
said

psalm #2

tabletops
work
just
as
fine
as
a
drum
machine
when
used
correctly

hair

cutting a woman's dreads
is nothing like the shearing
i subject my own head to
the old familiar sting
of vibrating metal on skin
using a mirror as a guide
on this weekly journey

upon request to do so
i take a breath and close my eyes
and nod to myself
that all will be okay when it's over

one by one
i traverse her scalp
rolling each lock between fingertips
"only ma nature can weave like that"
i whisper just over her left ear
she hears me and turns slightly

i lean out
gently and firmly place the cold steel
to one of the nappy constellations
trying in vain not to notice in the mirror
her eyes hiding behind trembling lids

it is thick and beautiful
rolling like the bluegrass country sides off 421
serpent mound round ground
from chocolate to dirty southern blonde
this rope is painted
i continue squeezing scissors tighter
between index and thumb
sitting awestruck at its resiliency
until each strand begins to give way
history is exposed
the everyday ins and outs
scents
sights
sounds
documented in each chapter of matted hair
i continue to cut

because
she
asked
me
to

waiting room meditation

truth proves nothing
even when shown
on t.v. screens over and over
truth is reduced to opinion

the truth is
that some opinions
don't matter
whether they're true
or not

kentucky. . .on my mind
(no place like home)

the sun is shining bright
and the morning declares
at its own pace
that it has arrived
and as i ascend from slumber
i take into lungs
breaths of bluegrass tinged vespers
that swirls as the day
continues to break and stretch
back into shape from the night before

what i see is a landscape that reminds me
of the bodies of bluegrass raised bonitas
rolling ground that reaches
from old man river
to coal mines in the appalachian foothills
the air here sways with swagger
that proves a divine presence
has taken up residence here

and here is where i am
a b-boy apostle
at home on stage with a mic in hand
or floating down the
western kentucky parkway
towards land between the lakes

my minds third eye opening wider
until every sight is a panoramic view
the ethereal essence
of this once dark and bloody ground
has descended through eons
aging like that honey brown elixir
does in charred oak
something is alive here
and it resonates through us all
and it is then i know
that i got kentucky on my mind

and during times of contemplation
this woodford county thoroughbred
has turned to the holy trinity for comfort
in the form of
mother nature
father time
and
a bottle of maker's mark
for once your respiration
includes the throaty aroma
of distilleries at work
sour mash syndrome
is capable of making bourbon
sound good damn near any time of day
or while toasting front porch nights on the hill
and early mornings on rooftops over the elkorn

my love runs
through this place like funny cide
did the first saturday in may

and maybe
if i lower
my lids
long enough
and expand my lungs
i can somehow
will this feeling
on a little past forever
because the sun
will always shine bright when
i've got kentucky on my mind

J O 493
(for mike)

my eyelids swell but are stubborn
holding fast against countless nights of desperation
as if named hoover/damned to an existence of agony
never giving way to what must happen
so my time here can go on without you

i sit
sometimes
as the young ones do
legs crossed pulled hangman's noose tight
to heaving chest that aches
this first day of the rest of my life
the earth from my vantage point
rolls with quietness
under a canopy of shaken and stirred air
and the aura of sadness that resides here
i pursue knowledge of self
and try to grasp a universal understanding
of human ways and questionable actions
but even after spilling what seems to be
an exxon valdez amount of ink
onto an infinite number of pages
i still have no idea
why it is that you are not here

i
wonder
if you ever hear my voice trembling
when i stand with your headstone before me
this period at the end of your sentence
is a reoccurring comma in my story
a story i never wanted to write
but ma nature and pa time saw fit
to slowly grind the very essence
of my souls' caverns
distilling the allusions i've created to cope
into an elixir for what is afflicting me
so many years after you've departed
physically from this place

i sometimes evoke your name
transplanting my present
back to when i was that child
whose eyes opened every morning
to search you out from all others
that would stand before me
i eager for big brother's acknowledgement
would hang from your words
while my imagination ran with the
possibility
of growing from child to man
running beside you instead of behind

the two of us barnstorming the bluegrass
not the little brother pursuing elder trails
like a bloodhound
not giving any thought to the
possibility
that my act of love
may be an annoyance
not a compliment
now baby brother has blossomed
becoming man child
often responding to others calls for you
you look just like your brother
they say briefly holding eye contact
trying to channel through my green mirrors
your mocha brown pools that
baptized your memory upon our brains
one simple glance at a time

confidants whisper to me
tapping the same rhythm over and over
it's   not   your   fault
but fault lines run deep
fissures running parallel to the silver lining
my future is supposed to have
now mornings are spent mourning
steeping the day with over a decades worth
of what ifs and i wish i mays
screaming at the universe
for one answer

one explanation
as to why you no longer are here
but some questions don't need answers
they must simmer down deep
at that subterranean level
bonding with every molecule
of every atom
that forms the fabric
that is sewn into every memory
i have of you
memories that both comfort and batter
leaving me with the will to persist
though my vision will always be
a bit blurry

about the author

Raised somewhere between the tobacco fields and horse farms of Woodford County, Kentucky, Jude McPherson has been bending and stretching syllables as long as he can remember. He blends his insatiable love of hip-hop with heaping helpings of front porch tall tales and social consciousness into his writing.

He has published two previous collections of poetry through blacoetry press; *loves taxicab blues revisited* (1998) and *the book of jude* (2000).

www.ingramcontent.com/pod-product-compliance
Lightning Source LLC
Chambersburg PA
CBHW051713040426
42446CB00008B/870